Written by Kim Sorgius

Graphic Design by Anne Villanueva

Edited by Lisa Walters

Contents

Developing a Quiet Time: A biblical study for kids

Day 1: Habits
Day 2: Good Morning, God!
Day 3: Read and Respond
Day 4: Open Heart Prayer
Day 5: Worship
Day 6: Scripture Memory
Day 7: Let's Review

Day 8: For Fellowship
Day 9: For Righteousness
Day 10: For Direction
Day 11: For Worship
Day 12: For an Example
Day 13: For a Witness
Day 14: Review

Day 15: The History of Quiet Time
Day 16: Does Time Matter?
Day 17: What Materials?
Day 18: Dealing with Distractions
Day 19: For When You Get Off Track
Day 20: About Prayer
Day 21: Review

Day 22: Joshua 1:8-9
Day 23: Romans 12:1-2
Day 24: James 1:22-23
Day 25: Philippians 4:8-9
Day 26: Matthew 5:1-12
Day 27: Psalm 139:1-14
Day 28: This is Not Goodbye

Habits

Do you want to be more like Jesus? I know I sure do. As a Christian, becoming more like Jesus is my #1 goal in life. Is it your #1 goal, too?

☒ YES   ☐ NO

This study is all about one of the most important ways that we can accomplish our goal of becoming more like Jesus: having a quiet devotional time with God. I'm so excited that you have joined me on this journey. We are going to learn a lot about why God wants us to have this quiet devotional time and how it will help us grow.

Some people call this time a quiet time and others call it a devotional time. Take a minute and write down everything that you know about having a quiet devotional time in this space below. We can use this at the end of the study to see how much you have learned!

Listening for guidance and understanding of the Holy spirit

From now on, I will call it a quiet time. If you prefer to call it something else, that is just fine!

A quiet time is simply an uninterrupted time with God. What do you think uninterrupted means?

Focusing on getting understanding of God's word

Having a quiet time in our world today is very hard to do. There is an endless list of distractions all fighting for our time and energy. We will talk more about those later. But first, let's talk a little more about what it is going to take to start having a quiet time on a regular basis.

What we really want is for our quiet time to become a habit.

Look up the word "habit" in the dictionary and write its meaning below.

a settled or regular tendency or practice or routine

A habit is something that we do often without even thinking much about it. Habits can be good things like reading your Bible every day, praying, or holding doors open for people. They can also be bad things like chewing with your mouth open, saying ugly words, or forgetting to turn off the light in your room.

Let's make a list of our good and bad habits in the chart below.

GOOD	BAD
Listening	
Helping People in need	

We are going to learn so much about what your quiet time might include, but for today let's just end by praying and asking God to open our minds and hearts to what He wants to teach us in this study.

Good Morning, God!

For our study, we will use the acronym "GROWS" to help us remember each part of our quiet time. The Bible has a lot to say about spending time with God, but it doesn't give us a specific formula. I want you to know that so you won't be confused about what we are doing in this study.

Often a quiet time will look very different from person to person. I think that God enjoys our creativity. However, since we are just starting out on this journey, I am going to teach you a specific formula that will help you remember the parts of a quiet time. These 5 parts are all wonderful ways to accomplish your goal of becoming more like Jesus.

The first letter in GROWS stands for Good Morning, God!

Good Morning, God!
Basically, we want to begin our quiet time by saying good morning to God. This could be a short little prayer or it could simply be the words "Good morning, God!"

Every morning when I wake up, the very first thing I say to God is good morning. He is my best friend and He is always there. I can't imagine not greeting Him! Take a minute and say good morning to God right now.

From now on whenever you see the "G for Good Morning God" I want you to write something that you said to God that morning. You may get ideas from the Good Morning God chart on page 1 of the appendix.

Go there now and write one for today.

Good Morning, God!

Thank you for Your Love, mercy and Grace

Read Psalm 143:8. Draw some things that make you filled with JOY this morning.

Let the morning bring me word of your unfailing Love, for I have put my trust in you. Show me the way I should go, for to you I entrust my life.

I'm going to tell you about each of the other parts of our GROWS formula this week. Until then, write a prayer to God below and tell Him how excited you are to be learning how to have a great quiet time with Him.

_____

_____

_____

_____

Read and Respond

Good Morning, God!

_____

Read and Respond

The R in GROWS stands for Read and Respond to God's Word. You will need your own Bible to do this. Just use any Bible around your house. It doesn't need to be anything specific.

Today, let's read Lamentations 3:21-23. Don't worry if you don't know where Lamentations is. With lots of practice you will know where to find each book. For now, you can find this one after Jeremiah, just a little past Psalms in the middle of your Bible. Or, you can always look in the table of contents in the front.

When you read these verses it's hard not to notice one thing about God. What do you see?

_____

_____

_____

I hope you could see God's love for you! It is faithful, never ending, and new every single morning. This is an important verse to start with because anytime you try to create a new habit, there will be times when you fail. I want you to commit to working in this study every single day. However, I know that sometimes you might forget or perhaps you will get busy. Sometimes you might sleep too late or simply forget to make God the priority of your day. That's OK. God still loves us when we do this. He wants us to keep trying and He promises that His mercies are new every single morning- even on mornings when we didn't spend time with Him!

How does that make you feel?

Are you ready to commit to (or promise) that you will work hard on making a quiet time a new habit in your life? Talk to your parents and decide if you will do it every single day or if you will do it every week day. Then write your commitment below.

_____

_____

_____

_____

Open Heart Prayer

Good Morning, God!

_____

Read and Respond

Have you ever heard of open heart surgery? It's pretty cool and pretty gross all at the same time. The doctors literally cut open a person's chest and open their heart in some way (depending on what is needed). The cool thing is that this surgery saves lives every single day.

I want you to think of prayer that way. First you must fully open your heart to God and second, you can rest assured that it will save your life! Let's take a minute and draw that thought here so we don't forget it:

Now read Psalm 139:23. What does David ask God to do?

_____

How does it make you feel when you think about God knowing your heart?

_____

_____

If you are like most people, that idea makes you very nervous because you know that you have sinned and that you aren't perfect. You know that your thoughts aren't always good thoughts. Just remember, that is exactly what David is telling God, too.

Read verse 24 now. What does David ask God to do?

_____

_____

One more thing. Read Jeremiah 17:9. What word does Jeremiah use to describe our heart? _deceitful + wicked_

Wow. Did you know how wicked your heart is? The world tells us every day to trust our heart, but we have to be very careful NOT to listen to this lie. AND now that we know this, it makes sense that praying can literally "SAVE OUR LIFE," right? By not trusting our heart and opening it up to God, we can make sure that we follow the right path. (Don't forget to check off the "R" for read and respond.)

Open Heart Prayer

Spend some time in open heart prayer now. Ask God to search your heart and to lead you down the right paths today.

Worship

Good Morning, God!

_____

Read and Respond

You probably know that we were created by God, but do you know why? Read Colossians 1:16. The very end of that verse makes it clear. Write your answer here:

_____

We were made FOR God, more specifically we were made to glorify and enjoy Him forever! Now, worship can take on many forms, but for this study we will use the word worship to talk about singing praises to God. (Psst… did you say good morning to God before you started this morning and did you check it off?)

Let's do a brief survey of Bible verses about singing praise to God. I want you to quickly read each verse and record a phrase or sentence telling what you learned about praise.

Psalm 95:1-2 _____

Psalm 147:1 _____

Psalm 104:33 _____

Psalm 150:6 _____

1 Chronicles 16:9 _____

Luke 19:40 _____

Open Heart Prayer

What a privilege it is to be able to praise God through song. Let's pray now and thank Him for this and ask Him to help us sing joyfully unto Him. Add requests/answers to your prayer sheet in the appendix.

Worship

Now that we know how important it is to worship God through song, let's do it!

For today, I want you to sing something you already know. If you don't know this song, sing something you do know, even if it's <u>Jesus Loves Me</u>. There is no need to fret about finding the perfect song for this time. Anything we sing to Him will be beautiful to His ears. Also, we don't need music. Just sing out with your voice and enjoy being with God!

God is so Good

God is so good. God is so good.
God is so good, He's so good to me.
He died for me. He died for me.
He died for me, He's so good to me.
He answers prayer. He answers prayer.
He answers prayer, He's so good to me.
I'll do His will. I'll do His will.
I'll do His will, He's so good to me.

Scripture Memory

Good Morning, God!

_____

Read and Respond

Good morning! (Did you remember to say good morning to God?) I am so excited about our last letter. Once we finish today, you will know all five parts of our quiet time formula. So let's get cracking!

Many people have a quiet time with God by reading His Word and praying. While that is a very good thing, I think there is one more very important part that can't be left out. We also need to be memorizing His Word. Let's read and see why.

Read Psalm 119:11. Why would we memorize God's Word?

_____

_____

Joshua 1:8 gives some benefits to memorizing God's Word. What are they?

_____

_____

Lastly, 1 Peter 3:15 gives us another very important reason to know Scripture. What is it?

_____

_____

If we are going to keep from falling in this world, we need Scripture. And as you noticed in that last verse, knowing Scripture will help us to tell others about Jesus. Not only do we want others to know this good news, Jesus left us with the command to share it with everyone!

Open Heart Prayer

Let's stop now and pray and ask God to help us memorize His Word and to put that desire in our hearts. Add requests/answers to your prayer sheet in the appendix.

Worship

Now sing God is so Good again today. Think about how good He really is to take the time to answer our prayers!

Scripture Memory

I'd like for you to memorize one verse for this study. I am assuming that you are memorizing other verses through your church, school work, and maybe even as a family. I don't want to add too much to that, but I do think this verse will be a really good one to know!

Look up Psalm 143:8 and write it below.

_____

_____

_____

_____

Let's Review

Good Morning, God!

_____

Read and Respond

Before we move on, let's take some time and review what we have learned. Fill in the space next to each letter telling the 5 parts of our quiet time.

G _____

R _____

O _____

W _____

S _____

Now let's read Ephesians 4:20-24. I want you to see that this passage describes our goal in quiet time.

What does verse 22 say that we are putting off or trying to get rid of?

_____

What does verse 24 say that we are trying to accomplish?

_____

I hope you can see that by spending time with God we are working to get rid of our old self (the one that is full of sin, evil, and corruption) and putting on our new self which is in the likeness of God.

When you became a Christian, you were given that new self. You didn't have to work for it. It was a free gift. If you haven't been given this gift and don't know Christ as your Savior, please talk to your parents or pastor today!

While this new self is a gift, Paul reminds us in the verse above that we must be "renewed in the spirit of our minds." He mentions this first in Romans 12:1-2. It seems like a hard concept to understand, but it's really quite simple.

Paul is talking about spending time with God through prayer, praise, and the reading of His Word. And this is what we are doing in our quiet time. It's no accident! We are purposely working to renew our minds so that we can be more like Christ.

Open Heart Prayer

Let's stop now and pray and ask God to help us memorize His Word and to put that desire in our hearts. Add requests/answers to your prayer sheet in the appendix.

Worship

Sing God is so Good.

Scripture Memory

Read your verse 3 times today (Psalm 143:8). Check off each box as you do it.

☐1 ☐2 ☐3

Before we end this day, let's go ahead and write out our commitment again. Just copy it right from Day 3. It will be good for us to write it again!

_____

_____

_____

For Fellowship

This week we are going to study the reasons why we should have a quiet time. I'm excited to show you these reasons. Sometimes when we don't understand why we should do something, it's hard to feel like doing it. I don't want that to happen to you, so let's dig in.

Good Morning, God!

_____

Read and Respond

It all starts at the beginning. You know, Genesis. God created a perfect world. He had perfect fellowship with Adam and Eve. This means that He talked to them and walked with them. Just one glance over Genesis 1 and 2 and you will see how often God talked to Adam.

And then in Genesis 3, everything changed. Adam and Eve both lost the ability to talk directly to God as a punishment for what?

_____

With the entrance of sin into the world, we lost what was most precious, fellowship with God. For thousands of years, the people of God struggled greatly with this. They wondered if He really heard them or if He would really help them. And because of all of this wondering, they often strayed away from God and began worshiping other gods.

Just read what God says about them in Exodus 32:9. What words does He use to describe the people?

_____

But there is good news. We don't have to live in the darkness where we no longer hear from God. Jesus was sent to this earth to bridge that gap for us. We now have the privilege of once again having this fellowship.

Read 1 Corinthians 1:9. We get this fellowship through whom?

_____

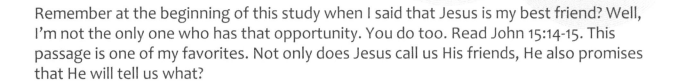

Remember at the beginning of this study when I said that Jesus is my best friend? Well, I'm not the only one who has that opportunity. You do too. Read John 15:14-15. This passage is one of my favorites. Not only does Jesus call us His friends, He also promises that He will tell us what?

_____

_____

Open Heart Prayer

Let's do that now. Stop for your open heart prayer and tell God everything that you are thinking and feeling about this study, about your day, about your family, about ANYTHING! Add requests/answers to your prayer sheet in the appendix.

Worship

Now let's move on to our worship. I'd like for you to learn the hymn What a Friend We Have In Jesus this week. Perhaps you already know it. If you don't, have your parents help you find it on the internet. The lyrics are provided at the end of this study for you.

Scripture Memory

Please write Psalm 143:8 below.

_____

_____

_____

_____

For Righteousness

Good Morning, God!

_____

Read and Respond

Have you ever played with a friend so much that your words or actions started to sound/look like theirs? _____ This is actually really common. In fact, it's the reason why your parents are always telling you to be careful who you pick to be your friends.

Read 1 Corinthians 15:33 and write it below.

_____

_____

As you can see, even if we feel like we are very strong Christians, the wrong friend (or company) can change who we are. Now you can see how wise your parents really are. But I want you to also think about it the other way around. If you spend time with someone who is a good example, what might happen?

_____

_____

Let's read 2 Timothy 3:16-17. Make a list of the things that our time in God's Word will be good for (hint: There are 4 things).

1. _____

2. _____

3. _____

4. _____

God uses His word to teach us, correct us, and prepare us to do the work that He has for us. He wants to help us become righteous. Which means, we need to read it, right?

Open Heart Prayer

Let's pray that God will use His Word in our hearts today to make us more like Him. Ask Him to teach you and prepare you to do the work that He wants you to do! Add requests/answers to your prayer sheet in the appendix.

Worship

It's time to sing! Turn to the back and sing <u>What a Friend We Have in Jesus</u> again today.

Scripture Memory

Write your Scripture memory here (Psalm 143:8). Challenge yourself to think of a few of the words before you look back at the Bible.

_____

_____

_____

_____

For Direction

Good Morning, God!

_____

Read and Respond

Let's start today by reading Psalm 25:4-5. These verses tell us another reason why we would want to spend time with God.

_____

_____

I hope you saw that if we spend time with God, He will show us which way to go. Have you ever had to decide whether or not you would hit your brother when he was being annoying? Or have you ever had to resist taking another cookie when no one was looking?

I bet you have faced a lot of difficult situations. We are much more likely to make a good choice in hard situations if we allow God to lead our paths. This goes back to what we said a few days ago about getting God's Word into your heart, too.

Starting your day with God can help you make good decisions all day long! Let's spend a minute and think about some decisions that we have made recently that we should have done differently.

THINGS I SHOULD HAVE DONE DIFFERENTLY

_____   _____

_____   _____

_____   _____

Open Heart Prayer

Ask God to help you rely on Him to direct your path and make good decision today. Ask Him to forgive you for the things that you listed above.

Worship

Sing <u>What a Friend We Have in Jesus</u>. Don't forget to sing like you mean it! Words are meaningless unless you truly sing from your heart!

Scripture Memory

Writing down Scripture is one of the best ways to memorize it. Let's write Psalm 143:8 again today.

_____

_____

_____

_____

For Worship

Good Morning, God!

_____

Read and Respond

People can be pretty selfish. That includes you and me. Often we will think about something like having a quiet time and the first question that comes to mind is, "How can this benefit me?" Or we might be tempted to think that God will be more likely to answer our prayers if we have a regular quiet time. We're selfish. Plain and simple.

While having a quiet time does have benefits for us, we must remember what we were created for. Write it here (see day 5) _____.

We were made to worship the Lord. We are not doing this quiet time thing to GET something from God. We are doing it to GIVE something to God. Well, not just something. We want to give God our everything.

Let's write Revelation 4:11 here today. While you are writing, really think about the words.

_____

_____

_____

_____

Open Heart Prayer

Now let's try something new for our open heart prayer time. I want you to pray the words of Revelation 4:11. Just read them and think about them like a prayer. God loves it when we pray using His Word! Add requests/answers to your prayer sheet in the appendix.

Worship

Sing <u>What a Friend We Have in Jesus</u>.

Scripture Memory

Write your Scripture Memory (Psalm 143:8) here. Except this time, just write every other word, leaving space for the missing words. Then close your eyes and try to say the verse. Read it in your Bible again, then close the Bible and try to fill in the missing words below.

_____

_____

_____

_____

For an Example

Good Morning, God!

G

_____

R

Read and Respond

Today let's read 1 Timothy 4:10-12. Paul is writing this passage to young Timothy. He wants to remind him that even though he is young, he is still to set an example for believers. Have you ever considered what example you might be setting? Write about the example that you are now below.

_____

_____

_____

It's likely that you weren't too impressed with what you wrote. But that's ok. Remember, we are in this to learn. What I want you to see today is that your life is an example whether it's a good one or a bad one. You are an example to younger siblings, older siblings, friends, and even your grandma or grandpa!

Look at that verse again and write down the 5 ways that we can be an example (hint: it's the last part of verse 12).

1. _____

2. _____

3. _____

4. _____

5. _____

Now that you have read this verse, what are some ways that you can be an good example to those around you?

_____

_____

_____

Open Heart Prayer

Pray now and ask God to help you be a better example to all of the people in your life. Name them specifically and also read over the last part of verse 12 as part of your prayer. Add requests/answers to your prayer sheet in the appendix.

Worship

Sing <u>What a Friend We Have in Jesus</u>.

Scripture Memory

Without opening your Bible, see how much of Psalm 143:8 you can write today. Don't be hard on yourself. Once you have finished go ahead and open the Bible and fix mistakes or fill in the parts you couldn't finish.

_____

_____

_____

_____

For a Witness

Good Morning, God!

_____

Read and Respond

Yesterday we talked about how our quiet time habits are an example to others in our life. But there is one more part of this that I want you to see. What was one of the last commands that Jesus gave to His disciples? Read Mark 16:15 for the answer.

_____

Read Psalm 96:3 and write it here:

_____

It's clear that God wants us to share the news of Jesus Christ, our Savior. But we can't do that if we don't know what to say. Remember 1 Peter 3:15? Let's read that again quickly. What does God want us to be ready for?

_____

If one of your friends were to ask you about Jesus, would you know what to tell them? Unless you are regularly studying God's Word, it will be hard to give an answer. Not only that, if we aren't experiencing fellowship with God our answer to them might be boring or flat sounding. Don't you want your friend to hear how wonderful a relationship with Christ truly is?

Open Heart Prayer

Let's pray today that God will help us to be ready to give an answer. Ask Him to prepare you and teach you as you study His Word. Ask Him to give you an opportunity to share with your friends, too! Add requests/answers to your prayer sheet in the appendix.

Worship

Sing <u>What a Friend We Have in Jesus</u>.

Scripture Memory

Today let's start learning the verse in phrases. This is one of my favorite tricks for Scripture memory. A phrase is just a short group of words that goes together. In Psalm 143:8, the first phrase might be this: "Let me hear in the morning of your steadfast love." That is what the ESV translation says. If you are using a different translation, that is fine. Just look for a way to break up the verse in 4 parts. (Ask your parents for help if needed.) Now write just part 1 on these lines (not the whole verse). Write it 4 times!

_____

_____

_____

_____

Review

Good Morning, God!

_____

Read and Respond

Let's review what we have learned this week. Look back and list the 6 reasons that we want to have a regular quiet time. (Hint: each of the last 6 days has given you one reason).

1. _____   4. _____

2. _____   5. _____

3. _____   6. _____

What verse did you read this week that meant the most to you? Write or draw about it below.

[ ]

Now let's end our study of this section with Psalm 73:25. Look it up and write it below.

_____

_____

Open Heart Prayer

Today pray and tell God all the reasons why you want to have a regular quiet time with Him. Specifically pray the words of Psalm 73:25 back to Him.

Worship

Sing What a Friend We Have in Jesus. Add this song to your song sheet in the appendix. While you are there, add the first song we sang, too. (God is so Good)

Scripture Memory

Write part 1 of your verse (Psalm 143:8) here today from memory:

_____

Did you get it right? ☐ YES   ☐ NO

If you did, go ahead and write out part 2 of your verse below. If you didn't, write part 1 again. Don't worry. Practicing Scripture is a wonderful thing. Do it as much as needed!

_____

_____

_____

_____

The History of Quiet Time

Good Morning, God!

_____

Read and Respond

In 1695 a humble pastor by the name of Thomas Ken wrote 3 hymns for the boys who were students at his college. The hymns were written for the boys to use as a part of their "quiet time." Each morning and evening they would sing the songs as part of their time with God. Those 3 songs all ended with the same chorus which is now known as the <u>Doxology</u>, one of the most famous hymns of all time.

When I first read this story I was fascinated to think that such a beautiful song had been originally written for the purpose of quiet time with God. And it reminded me that this idea is not new. In fact, Moses, David, and Joshua all have "quiet times" recorded in the Bible.

I have to say that I really love what Job had to say about spending time with God. Let's read Job 23:12. In this verse Job says that he treasures God's Word more than what?

_____

Wow. That's pretty serious. Do you think that you treasure God's Word as much as that?

_____

I have to admit that I would have a hard time saying that I do, at least much of the time anyway. And yet I think about the people around the world that do not have Bibles at all. Did you know about these people? Wycliffe Bible Translators says that over 180 million people still do not have a Bible in their language at all. And that doesn't even count the countries where it is illegal to be a Christian. We have a lot to be thankful for, don't we? Let's give thanks for the privilege of quiet time right now.

What is your favorite part of quiet time so far? Also write why you enjoy it.

_____

_____

_____

Open Heart Prayer

Pray and thank God that you have a Bible and the opportunity to read it. Pray for those who do not have that chance because there isn't a Bible in their language or because their country does not allow them to have one. Add requests/answers to your prayer sheet in the appendix.

Worship

This week we will sing the <u>Doxology</u>. If you don't know it, please take the time to learn it. Ask your parents to help. The words are in the appendix of this study.

Scripture Memory

Write part 1 of Psalm 143:8 without looking:

_____

Write part 2 on each line (try not to look):

_____

_____

_____

Does Time Matter?

Good Morning, God!

_____

Read and Respond

Whenever someone starts talking about having a quiet time, people seem to have the same questions. Do I have to do it in the morning? Do I have to do it every day? How long do I have to do it?

Today I'd like to help you answer some of those questions. First it's important to recognize that these 3 questions might be showing a heart problem. Sometimes people call it an "attitude problem." It's important to remember that when it comes to God, you don't HAVE to do anything. He isn't going to force you to have a quiet time.

God wants us to choose Him. He won't force us. So the real question is, "Do you WANT to?" Hopefully after studying the benefits of a quiet time last week your answer is a definite YES!

While there is nothing forced about the quiet time, there are reasonable answers to the questions asked.

- **Do I have to do it every day?** No, but don't you want to do it as often as possible?
- **How long do I have to do it?** There is no time limit. Spend as much time with God as you'd like!
- **Do I have to do it in the morning?** No, you don't. BUT, there are some great benefits to doing it then.

Let's look at Mark 1:35. When did Jesus spend time with the Father?

_____

I believe that Jesus did this early in the morning for at least two reasons. First, He needed to get away from distractions (we will talk about that more this week). Also, He needed to prepare to walk with His Father that day.

Remember when we learned that our quiet time could help us stay on the right path? Getting God's direction for our day is a VERY good way to start it. Let's read Psalm 63:1-3. In the King James Version, it says that David seeks God early in the morning (your translation might say "earnestly").

Write some of the other things that you notice about this passage.

_____

_____

Let's read one more verse today. Turn to Matthew 6:33. When does it tell us to seek God?

_____

So that leaves us with 3 really good reasons to have our quiet time in the morning:
- It keeps us from distractions.
- It helps us to have direction for our day.
- It keeps our focus on God first.

Open Heart Prayer

Pray today and ask God to help you to have the right attitude about your quiet time. Ask Him to help you make the most of your day by starting it focused on Him. Add requests/answers to your prayer sheet in the appendix.

Worship

Sing the <u>Doxology</u>.

Scripture Memory

Write Part 1 of Psalm 143:8 here:

Write Part 2 here:

_____

Now practice writing part 3 on each line below:

_____

_____

What Materials?

Good Morning, God!

_____

Read and Respond

Today I want to talk to you about truth. Do you know how to know if something is true? Write your answer below.

_____

Let's see how the Bible answers that question. Look up each of these verses and write the main idea of the verse.

Psalm 119:160 _____

Psalm 33:4 _____

Proverbs 30:5 _____

2 Corinthians 1:20 _____

Hopefully you saw that they all shared one main idea- that God's Word is true. We can count on this 100% of the time. Look at John 14:6. Who is the truth?

_____

Now let's read Matthew 24:4-5. What is Jesus warning us to watch out for?

_____

It's sad, but true. Many people on this earth will try to trick you or teach you false information. Some do it on purpose and others don't even realize it. That's why we have been using the Bible for this study. I don't want you to trust me without opening the Bible and seeing for yourself that what I am teaching you is true!

Do you have to use the Bible only? No, not necessarily. But I want you to remember that if you are spending time in God's Word, it should be mostly if not completely in God's Word. Reading a story or a book ABOUT God's Word is not the same. And it's possible that it's not true.

There are lots of great resources out there to help point you to God, so don't think that the Bible is the only thing you should ever read again. Just remember that when you read ANYTHING other than God's Word, you should always compare the teaching in it to what is truly in God's Word.

Open Heart Prayer

Pray and ask God to help you to always see the truth. Ask Him to shield you from false teaching and those who want to lead you away from Him. Ask Him to help you to discern (or see clearly) when something is not true. Add requests/answers to your prayer sheet in the appendix.

Worship

Sing the Doxology.

Scripture Memory

Write Part 1 of Psalm 143:8 from memory :

_____

Write Part 2 from memory :

_____

Write Part 3 from memory:

_____

Write part 4 on each line (you may use your Bible):

_____

_____

_____

Dealing with Distractions

Good Morning, God!

_____

Read and Respond

A few days ago we talked about how Jesus went out early in the morning before it was light to pray. We said that it was likely that one of the reasons He did this was to avoid distractions. Have you ever felt distracted while reading the Bible or working on something else? Write about that below:

_____

_____

There are so many things in this world that might distract us. Circle the ones in the list below that distract you most often.

phone	TV	sister
brother	music	pets
noises	hunger	too much to do
other animals	video games	toys
parents	friends	money
clothes	hairstyles	internet

That's a lot of distraction and it's really just the beginning. As you get older, the list will get longer and longer.

So if our lives are so distracting we know that we need to be diligent to have our quiet time with God BEFORE our life begins each day, right? _____

Otherwise, we will be fighting off siblings, animals, hunger, and many other things while trying to get our quiet time done. There is one more strategy that we can use to fight the distractions.

Read Isaiah 26:3 today. In this verse there is a promise. What is the promise to us?

_____

And what do we need to do to get this "perfect peace" that is promised?

_____

Tip: Have all of your quiet time materials together in your room. Before you leave your room in the morning, have your quiet time. If you share a room with your siblings, ask your parents to help you find a place where you can do your quiet time without distractions. Some people even use a closet! You can keep your materials together in a basket to carry to your special place if needed.

Open Heart Prayer

Say a prayer today asking God to help you keep your mind focused on Him so that you can have peace from all the distractions of this world. Ask Him to help you remember to start your day each day with quiet time with Him. Add requests/answers to your prayer sheet in the appendix.

Worship

Sing the Doxology.

Scripture Memory

Write as much of your verse (Psalm 143:8) from memory as possible . Then count how many words you got by yourself. Finish anything you forgot by checking the Bible.

Words correct _____

_____

_____

_____

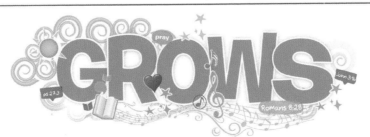

For when you get off track

Good Morning, God!

_____

Read and Respond

Do you remember when we read Lamentations 3 at the very beginning of this study? I reminded you that God's mercies are new every morning- even on days when we mess up! I started the study with that verse because I knew that there would be times that you would forget your quiet time or possibly even not feel like doing it.

Have you forgotten or neglected to do your quiet time since we started? Write about how it made you feel.

_____

_____

It's really easy to get discouraged when we get off track. In fact, we start lying to ourselves and saying things like, "I'm never going to get this right" or "I shouldn't have even tried to do this." Don't believe these lies!

You and I are both going to fail many times in our lives. We are going to get off track with quiet time, maybe church attendance, and even more. The worse thing we can do is give up.

So today let's look up a few verses that tell us the TRUTH about this matter. Write what you learn from the verses below.

Philippians 4:13 _____

Matthew 19:26 _____

Galatians 6:9 _____

See what I mean? Nothing is impossible with God! He gives us the strength we need to do it and if we give up, we will not reap the harvest. Now since you probably aren't a farmer, let me tell you what that means. The harvest is the time when the farmer gets to pick and enjoy all of the crops that he worked hard to plant.

What Galatians is saying to you is that if you don't give up, you will get to enjoy the things that come with all of that hard work. Spending time with God is worth it!

Let's look at one more verse. Read Isaiah 41:10. What will God do for you? (Hint: there are 3 things mentioned.)

_____

This is one of the most encouraging verses I know. We don't have to be strong ourselves. God will strengthen us and help us. Don't give up on quiet time, ever! Even if you go through times when you don't do it, jump right back in and let God hold your hand through it!

Open Heart Prayer
Pray and ask God to strengthen you and help you to stay strong with your quiet time and to not ever give up (just like Isaiah 41:10 says). Add requests/answers to your prayer sheet in the appendix.

Worship
Sing the Doxology.
_____

Scripture Memory
Write out your whole verse (Psalm 143:8) from memory and see how much you can write from memory.

Words correct _____

_____

_____

_____

_____

About Prayer

Good Morning, God!

_____

Read and Respond

Today I'd like to talk to you a little about prayer. The truth is, we could do an entire month long study on this topic it's such a big one. But we are going to just spend a little time today to remember a few important things about prayer.

Tell me what you know about prayer. Do you have to close your eyes? Be in a particular place? How often should you do it?

_____

_____

One of the first verses about prayer that people think of is 1 Thessalonians 5:17. Read it and write it here.

_____

To pray without ceasing means to do it all the time. This verse makes clear that God doesn't need for us to be on the floor kneeling by our bed with our eyes closed and hands folded every time we pray. Of course, there is nothing wrong with any of that. It's great to focus our thoughts by closing our eyes and to bow in respect for God. But we don't have to do that EVERY single time. Sometimes prayer is just a little "Good morning, God" or a whisper of thanks when He brings something nice our way.

Read Philippians 4:6. This is another very popular verse about prayer. Let's look closely for these answers. What does the first phrase say?

_____

Depending on your version it tells us to be "careful" or "anxious" for nothing. That means that we are not to worry. Why aren't we to worry? Well, the rest of the verse tells us.

Instead of worrying, what does God want us to do? _____

How many things should we pray about? _____

We should always pray WITH what? _____

Hopefully you saw that God wants us to pray about everything and that He wants us to do it with thankfulness. This is one way we show Him that we trust Him.

There is no formula that we have to follow for prayer. However, many people use the word "ACTS" to remind them of the different parts.

A - adoration (praise to God)
C - confession of our sins
T -thanksgiving for what He has given us and done for us
S - supplication (asking Him to help us)

Whatever you do, spend some good quality time with God in prayer. Don't be in a hurry to finish up or just say a particular sentence because someone told you to. Talk to Him like a friend- because He is your friend!

Open Heart Prayer
Today let's pray using the ACTS formula that I showed you above. Tell God everything that is on your heart today! Add requests/answers to your prayer sheet in the appendix.

Worship
Sing the <u>Doxology</u>.

Scripture Memory
Write out your whole verse (Psalm 143:8) from memory and see how much you can get.

Words correct _____

_____

_____

_____

_____

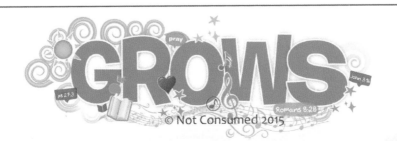

Review

Good Morning, God!

_____

Read and Respond

We've learned so much this week. I'm so proud of you for making it this far! We are going to review today with a crossword puzzle. Use the pages from this week or your Bible to find the answers.

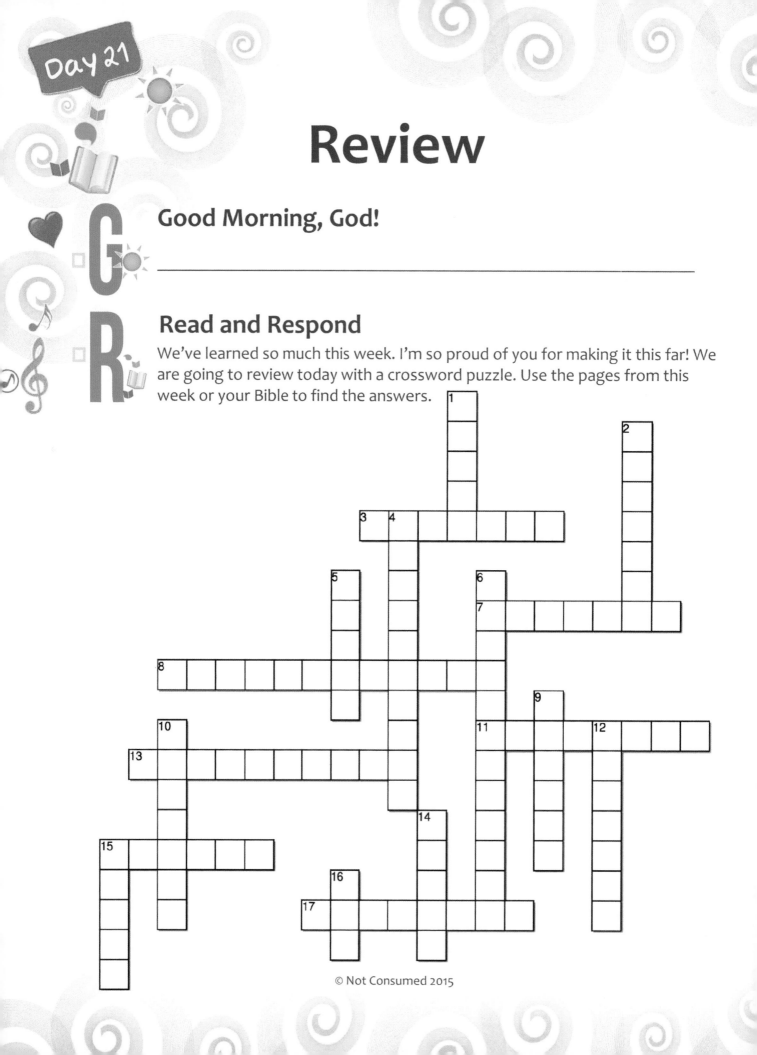

Across

3. 1 Thes. 5:17 says to pray without _____
7. If we don't give up, we will reap the _____
8. asking God to help you
11. Isaiah 41:10 says God will give you _____ .
13. telling God you are sorry for sinning
15. Jesus is my _____
17. hymn written for quiet time

Down

1. Who is the truth?
2. God's _____ are new every morning (Lam 3)
4. Phil 4:6 tells us to pray about ____
5. Isaiah 26:3 promises us perfect _____
6. telling God you are thankful
9. when we talk to God it's called _____
10. the best time of day for a quiet time
12. _____ is impossible with God.
14. the most reliable source of truth
15. when should we seek the kingdom of God
16. loved the Bible more than food

Open Heart Prayer

Pray today thanking God for teaching you so much through this study. Thank Him for something new that you learned this week. Add requests/answers to your prayer sheet in the appendix.

Worship

Sing the <u>Doxology</u>. Add this song to your song list in the appendix.

Scripture Memory

Write out your whole verse (Psalm 143:8) from memory and see how much you can get.

Words correct _____

_____

_____

_____

_____

Instructions for Week 4

This week we are going to do something totally different. It's time for you to try this quiet time thing on your own. I am going to give you 6 Bible study sheets to use. I will also tell you what passage to read. The rest is up to you.

Here is what you will need to do each day:

 - Use the appendix for ideas as usual

 - Using the passage I give you, complete the sheets on your own

 - Say your own prayer. Remember to add prayer requests and answers to your prayer list in the appendix.

 - Choose a song to sing each day. Add new songs to your song list. I have included a few ideas on the list for you.

- Choose one passage to memorize this week. If you can't think of one, do Joshua 1:9.

Passages for each day:
Day 22- Joshua 1:8-9
Day 23- Romans 12:1-2
Day 24- James 1:22-23
Day 25- Philippians 4:8-9
Day 26-Matthew 5:1-12
Day 27- Psalm 139:1-14

TODAY IS: __Day 22__

VERSES I READ TODAY: __Joshua 1:8-9__

_____

WHO IS IT ABOUT/FOR? _____

WHEN WAS IT TAKING PLACE? _____

WHAT IS THE PASSAGE SAYING? _____

_____

_____

HOW DOES THIS APPLY TO ME? _____

_____

_____

PRAYER NEEDS FOR TODAY

VERSES I AM MEMORIZING

OTHERS _____

_____

_____

_____

ME _____

_____

G.R.O.W.S.

WRITTEN THIS DAY: **Day 23**

WHAT I READ TODAY:
Romans 12:1-2

THIS PASSAGE MAKES ME THINK OF WHAT OTHER PASSAGE IN THE BIBLE

WHAT DOES THIS PASSAGE MAKE ME WANT TO CHANGE?

MY PRAYER TO GOD TODAY:

SCRIPTURE MEMORY

G.R.O.W.S

WHAT DOES THIS PASSAGE MAKE CLEAR TO ME?

TODAY IS: _Day 24_

ILLUSTRATE
THIS VERSE/PASSAGE:

James 1:22-23

SCRIPTURE MEMORY _____

_____

_____

_____

PRAYER
NEEDS FOR TODAY:

➡ OTHERS:

ME:

SCRIPTURE: Philippians 4:8-9

G·R·O·W·S

TODAY IS: Day 25

OBSERVATION:

APPLICATION:

PRAYER:

SCRIPTURE MEMORY _____

_____

_____

TODAY IS: **Day 26**

VERSES I READ TODAY:
matthew 5:1-12
_____

_____

_____

_____

G.R.O.W.S.

TRUTH FROM GOD'S WORDS

MY PRAYER LIST

_____

_____

_____

_____

_____

_____

SCRIPTURE MEMORY _____

_____

_____

G.R.O.W.S

WHAT I HAVE READ TODAY: Psalm 139:1-14

TODAY IS: Day 27

MY PRAYER

WHAT I HAVE LEARNED ABOUT GOD

SCRIPTURE MEMORY _____

_____

_____

This is Not Goodbye

We have come to the end of our study. For the last month, you have successfully created a quiet time with God. I'm so proud of you! How do you feel?

_____

_____

What was the biggest thing that you learned this month?

_____

_____

_____

We may be at the end, but this is not good-bye. You have learned a new habit that will be a part of your life forever! I would encourage you to continue using the GROWS formula to guide your quiet time. It's a great way to spend quality time with God.

Before we go, I'd like for you to look up one last verse: Hebrews 11:6. Write the whole verse below.

_____

It's not your effort in having a quiet time that pleases God, but your faith! Believing that God will meet you here each day, that He is your friend, and that He desires fellowship with you is what pleases Him. He loves you so much!

Take a few minutes now and write a prayer of commitment to God. Tell Him how thankful you are for the time that you spent with Him this month and ask Him to help you keep going every day from now on!

_____

_____

_____

_____

_____

_____

_____

_____

Appendix

Checklist   1

Ways to Say Good Morning   2

Prayer List   3

Song List   4

   Doxology   5

   God is so Good   6

   What a Friend We Have in Jesus   7

Scripture Memory   8

Good morning, God!

- Jesus, I adore you.
- My soul magnifies you Lord.
- Holy, Holy, Holy are you Lord.
- O Lord, everything in heaven and earth is yours.
- I love you Lord.
- Thank you, Lord, for saving my soul.
- This is the day that the Lord has made.
- Lord I love you with all my heart and with all my soul and with all my mind.
- Thank you that you are always with me.
- In the beginning was the Word, and the Word was with God, and the Word was God.
- I will praise you Lord for your mighty deeds.
- My spirit rejoices in God my savior.
- I can't wait to be with you today Lord.
- Thank you Lord for another beautiful day.
- Thank you for being my Savior.
- Lord, your Word is truth.
- Thank you for always loving me, Lord.
- Your mercies are made new every morning.
- The joy of the Lord is my strength today.

- How great thou art!
- Today I can smile because YOU saved me!
- Thank you for my family, Lord.
- Lord you are always faithful.
- My soul longs to be with you today, Lord.
- Thank you for being my strength today, Lord.
- I trust you, Lord.
- Thank you for directing my paths, Lord.
- Thank you that you never change, Lord.
- I love to obey you, Lord.
- Thank you for a safe place to live, Lord.
- I can't wait to read your Word today, Lord.
- Thank you for being my friend, Lord.
- Lord, your plans for me today are good.
- Thank you that I have a Bible, Lord.
- Thank you for my church, Lord.
- Teach me today, Lord.
- Lord, you are so good.
- I need you every hour, Lord.
- I delight to do your will today, Lord.

Open Heart Prayer

Request	Answer

Worship

♪ Jesus Loves Me

♪ Amazing Grace

♪ Isn't He Wonderful

♪ Praise the Lord Together

♪ I Have Decided to Follow Jesus

♪ Fairest Lord Jesus

♪ Trust and Obey

♪ Holy, Holy, Holy

♪ Oh How He Loves You and Me

♪ _____

♪ _____

♪ _____

♪ _____

♪ _____

♪ _____

♪ _____

♪ _____

♪ _____

♪ _____

♪ _____

♪ _____

♪ _____

♪ _____

♪ _____

♪ _____

♪ _____

Worship

Doxology

Praise God, from whom all bles-sings flow; Praise Him, all crea-tures here be-low;

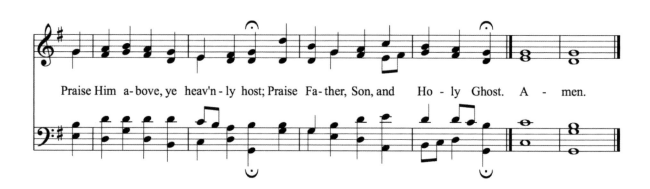

Praise Him a-bove, ye heav'n-ly host; Praise Fa-ther, Son, and Ho-ly Ghost. A - men.

Worship

God is So Good

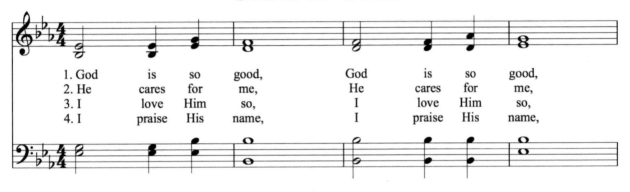

1. God	is	so	good,	God	is	so	good,
2. He	cares	for	me,	He	cares	for	me,
3. I	love	Him	so,	I	love	Him	so,
4. I	praise	His	name,	I	praise	His	name,

God	is	so	good,	He's	so	good	to	me!
He	cares	for	me,	He's	so	good	to	me!
I	love	Him	so,	He's	so	good	to	me!
I	praise	His	name,	He's	so	good	to	me!

Worship

What a Friend We Have in Jesus

1. What a friend we have in Je - sus, all our sins and griefs to bear!
2. Have we trials and temp-ta - tions? ____ Is there trou-ble a - ny- where?
3. Are we weak and hea - vy la - den, cum - bered with a load of care?

What a pri - vi-lege to car - ry eve - ry-thing to God in prayer!
We should ne - ver be dis - cour - aged; take it to the Lord in prayer!
Pre - cious Sav-ior still our ref - uge— take it to the Lord in prayer!

Oh, what peace we of - ten for - feit, oh, what need-less pain we bear,
Can we find a friend so faith - ful who will all our sor-rows share?
Do thy friends des-pise, for - sake thee? Take it to the Lord in prayer!

all be-cause we do not car - ry eve - ry-thing to God in prayer!
Je - sus knows our eve-ry weak - ness; take it to the Lord in prayer.
In his arms he'll take and shield thee; thou wilt find a so-lace there.

Scripture Memory

Instruction: Fill out your verse once you have memorized it!

_____

_____

_____

_____

Psalm 143:8

61757323R00038

Made in the USA
Charleston, SC
26 September 2016